For my mother and father.

--J.S.

For Uncle C., Uncle G., and Aunt Pinkie.

-- M.S.

Going Rouge: The Sarah Palin Rogue Coloring & Activity Book

By Julie Sigwart and Micheal Stinson

Illustrations by Julie Sigwart

Website: http://www.goingrouge.net

For volume discounts and wholesale, contact GoingRouge2012@gmail.com

Printing History:

November 2009:   First Edition

ISBN: 978-0-615-33277-2

Perfect holiday gifts for all the "Sarah's Rogues" on your list!

Word Salad Speech Generator Snow Globe

Sarah Palin Sellout Snow Globe

Put lipstick on these full lips then connect the dots to see what you've made!

**HINT: What's the diference between a Hockey Mom and a Pitbull?
The Pitbull doesn't quit.**

Help Sarah find her way to the White House!*

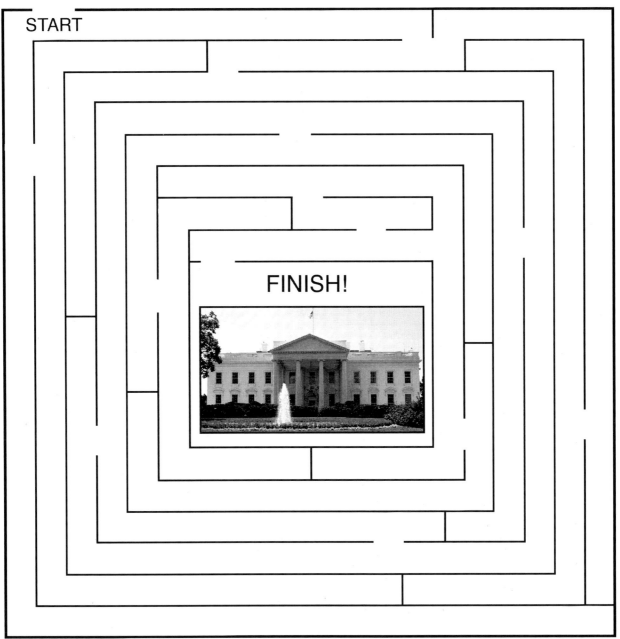

START

FINISH!

* If you find yourself in too deep or have more pressing concerns, you can always quit.

Pray with Sarah and help her go green by coloring the money.

What will Sarah's carbon footprint be after she burns through all that green?

It's Geography Time!
Sarah wants you to color the capital of Africa!

Sarah wants to go fishing. Help her choose the best gear for the job and color the page.

A.

B.

C.

D.

Sarah wins nomination for Prez! Who will she pick for her Veep?

HIGH SCHOOL BFF
CHENEY
JOE THE PLUMBER
TINA FEY
BABY JESUS
CANADA OIL MINISTER
A RAVING LUNATIC
RUSH LIMBAUGH
MANICURIST
WITCH DOCTOR

TODD'S BIZ PARTNER
MCCAIN
BOBBY JINDAL
STEPHEN COLBERT
HILLARY CLINTON
HELEN THOMAS
LEVI JOHNSTON
HAIR STYLIST
PREZ OF EXXON

```
T O D D S B I Z P A R T N E R J C
O G O D S B A B Y J E S U S P O A
H I L L A R Y C L I N T O N R E N
S T E P H E N C O L B E R T E T A
M C C A I N S U C K S T O A Z H D
A R A V I N G L U N A T I C O E A
N W E D S T O D D T O D D A F P O
I I N D N O T S N H O J I V E L I
C T E D S A R A H P A L I N X U L
U C H E L E N T H O M A S E X M M
R H C D S B D D O T O D D E O B I
I D H A I R S T Y L I S T Y N E N
S O E L V I S L I V E S D G E R I
T C N H G U A B M I L H S U R A S
O T E L A D N I J Y B B O B H S T
D O Y T I N A F E Y T O D D A S E
D R H I G H S C H O O L B F F O R
```

Sarah and Her Friends
Are Takin' Back America!

Finish the sentence by filling in the missing word!

ROGUE   ROGUE
OFFICE   BUDDY
ROGUE   MILLION
APPOINT WOOTEN
FIRE   ROGUE

1. Will you _____ Wooten already?

2. Meet Todd in my _____ even though he's not governor.

3. If I call Wooten _____ enough he'll be stuck in a desk job.

4. Maybe I should call Monegan _____ too, and ruin his career?

5. I can always _____ a high school _____ to your job.

6. I need a new _____ skin rug for my den.

7. Don't make me force my staff to call your office, like, a _____ times!

8. My branding you as a _____ cop is keepin' me from official duties.

9. Being _____ is tough, eh? Made millions myself, doin' it.

Color, cut out, and make your own Sarah Palin slogan and campaign buttons!

Sarah's Secret Recipe for Moose ala Palin!

For this recipe you'll need two snowshoes, a down jacket, a pole drag, a 30-06 rifle, a sharp bowie knife, and pure guts, *you betcha!*

First ya gotta getcher moose, a little olive oil, some parsley, salt and pepper, along with a whoppin' big cast iron fryin' pan.

Here's how ya do it, ladies: After being dropped off on a glacier via bush pilot, I erected a shelter from a crashed plane, started a fire and took a nap, (you gotta have that beauty rest, girls, if you expect to keep a big hunky man like Todd around). You betcha I dreamed of taking down a huge studly moose, what girl doesn't? Soon I was creeping through the bushes, slow, like a starvin' indian does it, and dear lord if I didn't come upon a perfect specimen, a mountain of a moose!

I popped a bullet right in the sweet spot, between the ribs, and only had ta track him for 7 miles or so before he heaved up enough blood to make him think about goin' ta heaven, while sittin' on his ribcage as he died so as to speed up the process, I don't have all day, hungry mouths to feed, and lots of 'em.

The worst part about field dressin' a 1500 lb moose in the middle of nowhere are those pesky wolves, jumpin' in, snappin' atcha, until you end up having to shoot them dead just to shut 'em up! Fish n Game guys was supposta kill 'em and save me the trouble, but no, there they were, hornin' in on my meat for the winter. My Thompson submachine gun made mincemeat out of them in short order, and soon I was up to my elbows in moose blood again. Had to cut them legs off, by golly, lose the head, toss the guts, and quarter what was left.

Which left me, myself and I to do the dirty work of packin' out about 800 lbs of raw meat, so I shouldered the load and made my way down the mountain, stole a native canoe and followed the river for 1800 miles to Anchorage, where I called a cab and brought home the moose bacon for thewhole family. Just another day in the Palin household, and now I need ta shower the guts off me. and, what self respectin' pioneer woman wouldn't?

Oh! *The RECIPE?!*

Wouldn'tcha know it? It's TODD's turn to do the cookin'!

Sarah the Huntress

1. Which creature did Sarah NOT kill and skin in 2008?

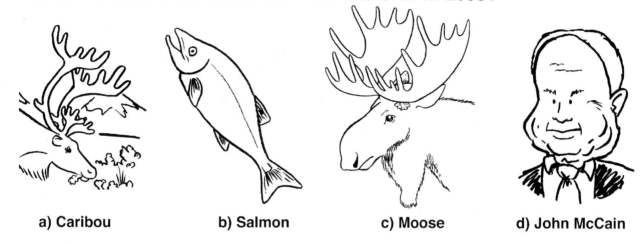

a) Caribou   b) Salmon   c) Moose   d) John McCain

2. What is Sarah guaranteed to take a stab at in 2012?

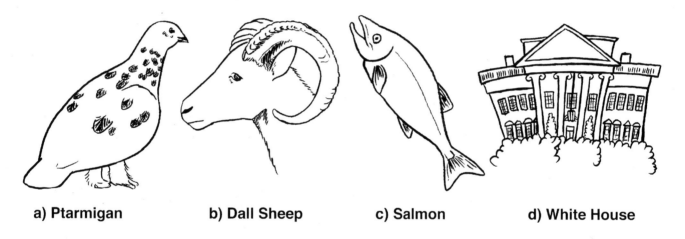

a) Ptarmigan   b) Dall Sheep   c) Salmon   d) White House

3. What animal will Sarah kill in 2012?

a) Moose   b) Caribou   c) Dall Sheep   d) Republican Party

Anagram Time!

Rearrange the letters below to form as many anagrams
as possible. We'll give you a few to get you started!

ENVIRONMENTAL ARMAGEDDON

A Dreamland Gnome Inventor

A Managed Lord Environment

A Melodrama Grind Nonevent

King Salmon for Dinner? You betcha!

Sarah got her lipstick mixed up with her bullets! Help her find it and color it rouge so she doesn't load it into her gun!

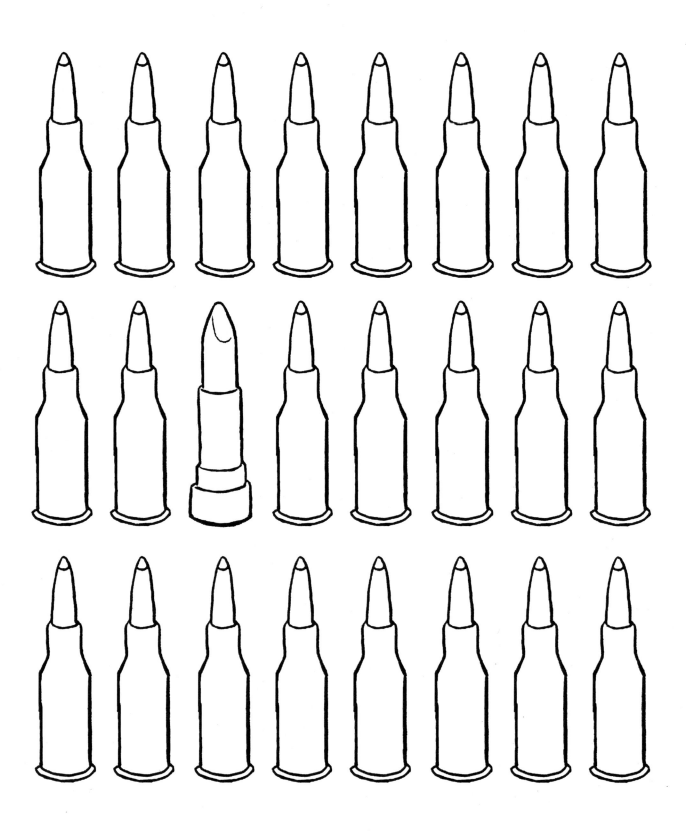

Sarah can see the end of the GOP from her house!

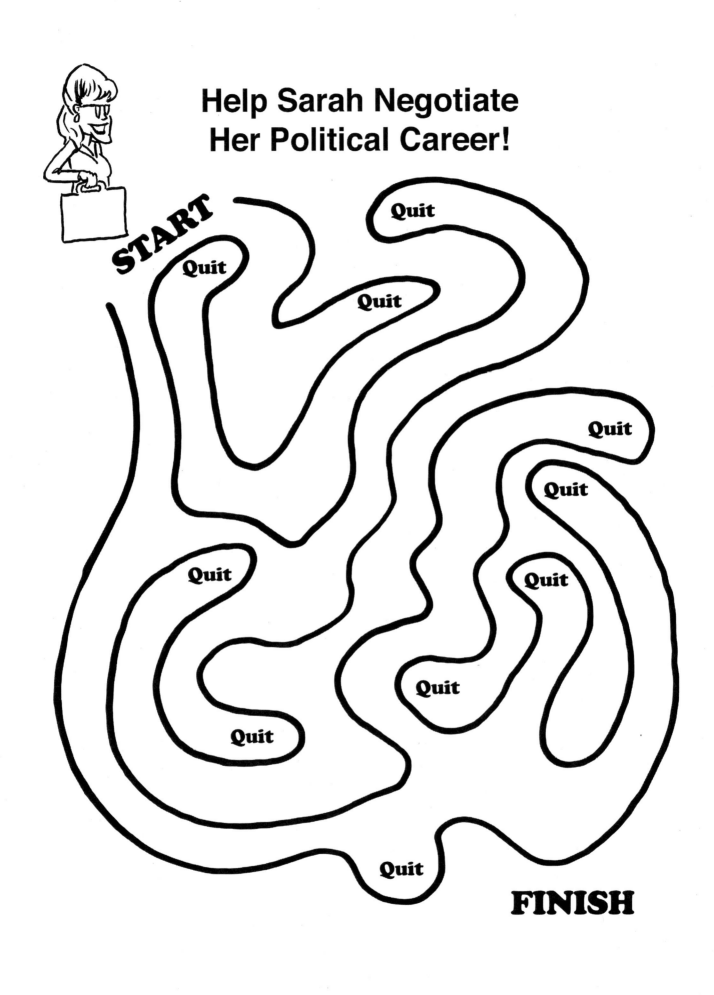

It's Geography Time Again!
Color the Nation that Doesn't Think Sarah is a Laughing Stock!

Unscramble the Words and Finish the Sentence!

1) tiuwaK   2) dgEenredna   3) egruo   4) mgriarae   5) tamiocnatoni

6) toansimerci   7) naNtlaio   8) csensiissoet   9) srainthiC   10) liasWal

1) Sarah visits _____ ; encourages Alaska big game hunting to troops. (Sep 2007)

2) Sues federal EPA for misusing ─────────────── Species Act. (Jan 2009)

3) "We cannot meet _____ leaders without conditions." (Sep 2008)

4) Officiated a _____ in the aisle of Wal-Mart. (Sep 2008)

5) Opposed protections for salmon from mining _____ (Aug 2008)

6) Strongly supports teaching _____ alongside evolution in schools:

7) Declare a _____ Day of Prayer in Alaska. (Apr 2008)

8) Claims to have never been part of an Alaska _____ party. (Sep 2008)

9) Recognize America's historic and founding _____ heritage. (Sep 2007)

10) Rejected making _____ bars close earlier than 5 AM:

Source: http://www.ontheissues.org/sarah_Palin.htm

Draw Sarah Palin
in Three Easy Steps!

Step 1:

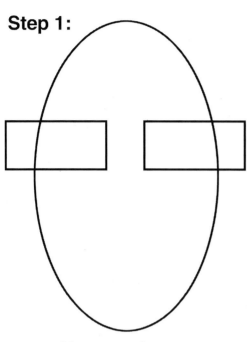

You can quit now.

Step 2:

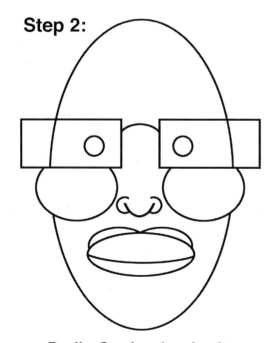

Really. Go ahead and quit.

Step 3:

So quit already! I mean it.

Color the Person Some Alaskans Considered the "Shadow Governor!"

The Tao-in of Palin
Search the puzzle and circle some of Sarah's favorite activities.

CRAZYMAKIN'
NEOCON-IN'
BITCHIN'
CUTTIN'
REVENGIN'
BLUFFIN'
DIVERTIN'
SLAYIN'
CONFUSIN'
REVOLTIN'
INGRACIATIN'

NEPOTISM-IN'
BABBLIN'
STUPIFYIN'
REVELATIN'
DISTORTIN'
DELUDIN'
CASHIN'
SPEAKIN' IN
   TONGUES
WINKIN'
TWITTERIN'

WOLF KILLIN'
FRAUDIN'
SUCKIN'
WAVIN'
RESIGNIN'
SECEDING'
ROGUE-IN'
TELEPROMPTERIN'
QUITTIN'
BLITHERIN'
CAMPAIGNIN'

```
R O G U E I N M E N I T T I U Q T
E S H O O T I N D E E D W N D C E
S E C E D I N W A V I N I G I R L
I B A R I B A B B L I N T R S A E
G I M E V S U C K I N X T A T Z P
N T P V E D E L U D I N E C O Y R
I C A E R B L U F F I N R I R M O
N H I N T X C U T T I N I A T A M
O I G G I C O N F U S I N T I K P
N N N I N E O C O N I N Z I N I T
I I I N N S T U P I F Y I N I N E
K F N O O C A V I N I T L O V E R
N E P O T I S M I N C A S H I N I
I F R A U D I N R E V E L A T I N
W O L F K I L L I N K S L A Y I N
S P E A K I N I N T O N G U E S O
B L A B B I N H B L I T H E R I N
```

Unscramble the Sarah Quotes*

"I think on a national level your Department of Law there in the White House would look at some of the things that we've been charged with and automatically throw them out."

ABC News interview, July 7, 2009

_____

_____

_____

"How sad that Washington and the media will never understand; it's about country. And though it's honorable for countless others to leave their positions for a higher calling and without finishing a term, of course we know by now, for some reason a different standard applies for the decisions I make."

Sarah Palin, July 4, 2009

_____

_____

_____

_____

"Personally, I've always been really interested in the ideas too about the land bridge. Ideas that maybe so long ago, had allowed Alaska to be physically connected to this part of our world so many years ago. My husband and my children, they're part [unintelligible] Eskimo, Alaskan natives. They're our first people, and the connection that may have brought ancestors from here to there is fascinating to me."

Sarah Palin, Hong Kong, Sept, 2009

_____

_____

_____

_____

*Don't feel bad, we couldn't do it either. You can always quit, ya'know.

Sarah wants a new doorknocker for her big house! Help her choose one!

ANTIQUE AMERICAN

OOSIK SPLENDOR

FRENCH CLASSIQUE

WOLF-NAIL COMBO

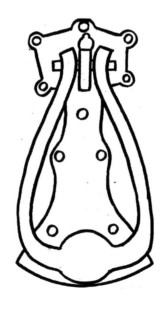

WESTERN STIRRUP

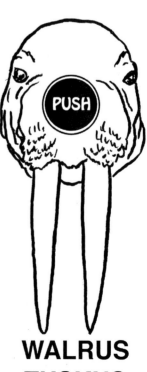

WALRUS TUSKUS

Copy each piece into the matching grid square to reveal the mystery picture!

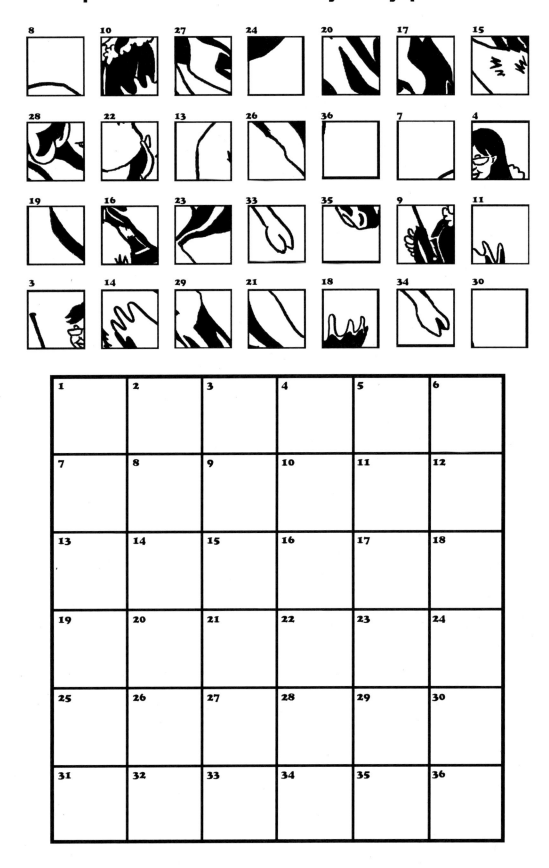

Sarah Keeps an Eye on Russia while She's Fixin' to do Some Chores! Color Sarah Red!

The Wolf Paw was
hung on the tree with
great care...
In hopes that the bounty
soon would be
theirs.

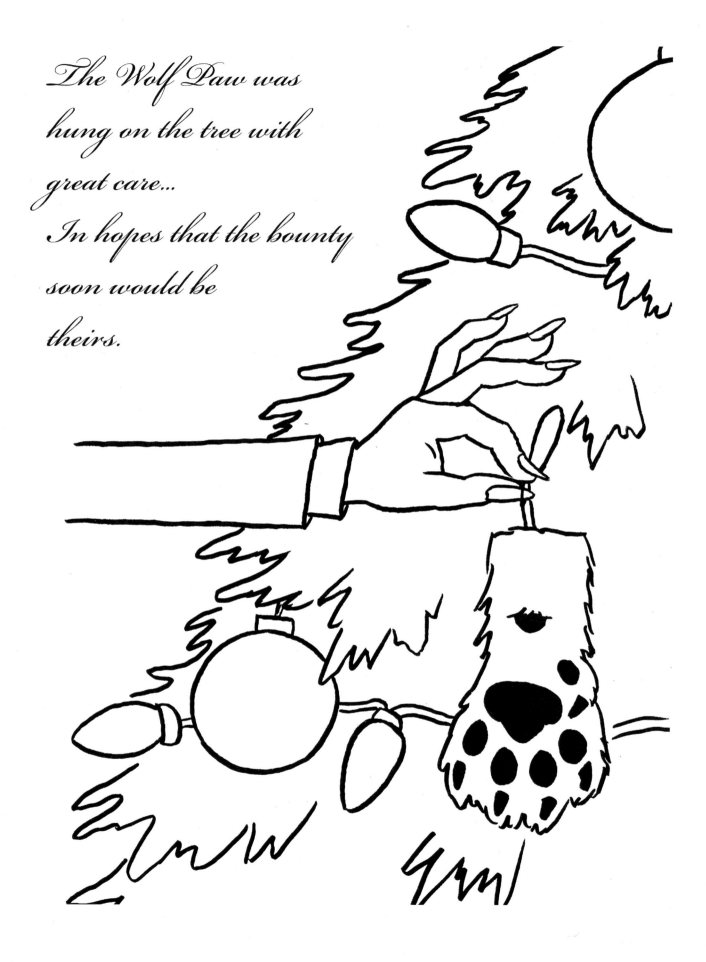

Carefully study the pictures of the caribou gracefully grazing in ANWR and circle the one that is different! Color the pictures!

The chilling coincidences between Abe Lincoln and Sarah Palin:

Both ate meat.

Both left office early.

Both wore "long johns" to be more liked by the guys.

Both used heavy mascara.

Both are easy on the eyes, if you know what I mean.

Both had missionary sex, but only to make babies.

Both picked teeth with a quill.

Both thought witch doctors were pretty handy to have around.

Both love hockey, and funky hats.

Both ran for office against corruption, refused state private jet use.

Both slaved over a hot stove, with no appreciation from the kids."

Both thought their Todd was a "hunky guy."

Both were so "mavericky" that it bordered on "roguey."

Both believed in gun safety.

Both shopped like there was no tomorrow.

Both plucked their beards.

Both were stone cold bitches if need be.

Both built a home with no money.

Both have chiseled faces that have been on a mountain.

Both said, "You betcha!" a lot, and ended speeches with a saucy wink.

Both wanted to be President really, really bad.

At the end of the day, nothing says secede -- er, *success* -- like a cup of tea.

Crossword Puzzlin' Time!

ALASKA

ACROSS

2 Supported this
4 ____ Palin
6 Legacy as Wasilla Mayor
9 ____ Palin
11 Drill, baby, drill here
12 Only a dead fish goes with the ____.
14 Wakes up each day, thinks of him, cries
15 Wanted to Declare a ____ Day of Prayer IN Alaska
20 Sent video message welcome as Gov to Alaska ____ party
22 Didn't write this either
24 "Meth Capitol" of Alaska
25 Unknown to Palins
29 Opposes ____ stem cell research
30 Cold War is "Off the table" with ____.
32 Will not meet rogue leaders without ____.
34 What Todd can't keep in his pants
35 Investigated for firing him
38 ____ Palin
39 Non-support of ____ marriage
40 Newpapers that Sarah reads

DOWN

1 When Putin rears head he goes into Alaskan ____.
3 Mantra
5 Alaskan currency
7 Love of Todd's life
8 In Wasilla they smoke
10 Lift moratorium on offshore
13 What Bristol is, per mom
16 Ghost written
17 Believes humans co-existed with
18 Sarah says NOT endangered
19 Told the Media to quit makin' this up
21 Supports teaching this design in public schools
23 He declared Sarah to be his Soul Mate
25 When she knows what it is, agrees with
26 Walrus likes to get a little mud on this
27 Bitter person clinging to guns and ____.
28 Short for Alaska Independence Party
31 Will wave/wink for money
33 ____ Palin
36 Newpapers that Sarah reads:
37 Harvest fish

Color the parts of Sarah's brain she uses the most. Color Sarah, too.

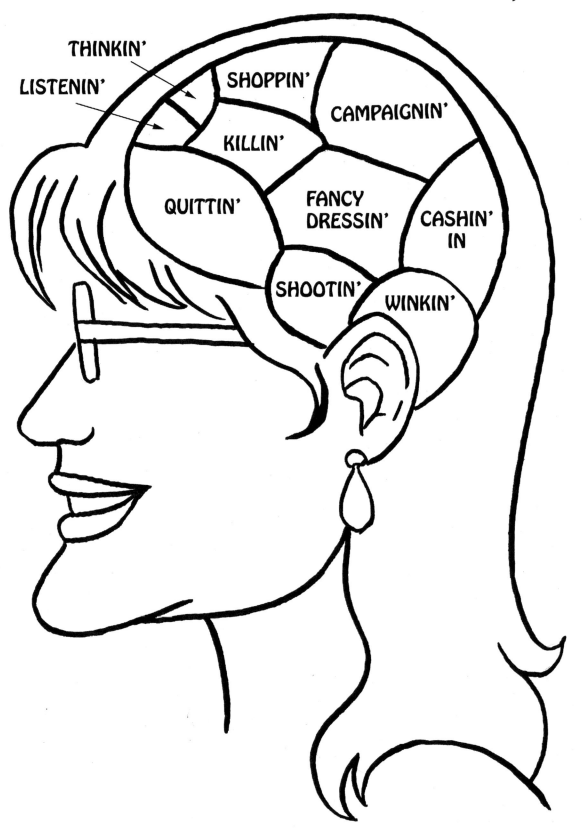

Some of Sarah's Favorite Alaskan Animals!
Match the items in the left to corresponding items in the right column. Draw a line between them!

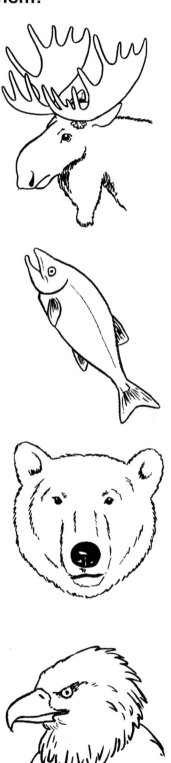

Match the Letters to the Numbers
to see Sarah's Secret Message!

1=a
2=b
3=c
4=d
5=e
6=f
7=g
8=h
9=i
10=j
11=k
12=l
13=m
14=n
15=o
16=p
17=q
18=r
19=s
20=t
21=u
22=v
23=w
24=x
25=y
26=z

__ __ __ __   __ __ __ __   __ __ __ __ __ __ __
9 7 15 20   13 9 14 5   19 21 3 11 5 18 19

__ __ __ __ __ __   __ __ __   __ __ __
13 3 3 1 9 14   23 1 19   20 8 5

__ __ __ __ __ __   __ __   __ __ __ __ __ __ __
2 18 9 4 7 5   20 15   14 15 23 8 5 18 5

__ __ __ __ __   __ __ __ __   __ __ __ __ __
19 16 5 14 4   2 1 21 25   19 16 5 14 4

__ __ __ __ __ __ __   __ __ __ __   __ __   __ __ __ __ __
7 12 1 19 19 5 19   13 1 11 5   13 5   19 13 1 18 20

__ __ __ __ __   __ __ __ __ __   __ __   __ __ __ __
23 8 9 20 5   8 15 21 19 5   15 18   2 21 19 20

Which one of these things does not produce a profit and must be crushed?

Oil Pipeline

Nuclear Power

Chemical Plant

Mountaintop Removal, "Clean" Coal

Hydro Power

Pristine Wilderness

Put lipstick on all the pigs! Is there enough for them all?

Sarah says, "Global Warming Affects Alaska but is not man-made."

Todd and Sarah are so proud of the witty names they've dreamed up for their children! Which of these names are not a Palin name?

TINA FEY
RICHIE RICH
WRAP THAT RASCAL
TRY BIRTH CONTROL
TRIG
TWITTER QUITTER
JESUS H. CHRIST
AIP

HILLBILLY
BOOGA BOOGA
BUDDHA
CASH 'N CARRY
LOCK AND LOAD
TRACK ENFIELD
SHOTGUN WEDDING
POLITICAL PROP

KILLA FROM WASILLA
SARAH JR.
BRISTOL
SLUSHY
IN MY CAR
WILLOW
PIPER

```
T I N A F E Y O B U D D H A O S K
W T R A C K E N F I E L D G O H I
I W P O L I T I C A L P R O P O L
T R Y B I R T H C O N T R O L T L
T A Y D B O O G A B O O G A O G A
E P G O D A I P S W I L L O W U F
R T H J E S U S H C H R I S T N R
Q H I I P A A O N A O A A I P W O
U A L I P F I O C I O I A I P E M
I T L P I P E R A P O P A I P D W
T R B I P T O O R H I L L O O D A
T A I N M Y C A R B I L L Y O I S
E S L I P E R O Y S L U S H Y N I
R C L O O F O B R I S T O L O G L
O A Y O O F O S A R A H J R I F L
D L R I C H I E R I C H T R I G A
L O C K A N D L O A D O O P R O P
```

Sarah's turkey pardon!

Dr. Rougelove

Or how I Learned to Start Worrying about the Mom

Answers

Help Sarah Choose her Vice President

```
T O D D S B I Z P A R T N E R J C
O G O D S B A B Y J E S U S P O A
H I L L A R Y C L I N T O N R E N
S T E P H E N C O L B E R T E T A
M C C A I N S U C K S T O A Z H D
A R A V I N G L U N A T I C O E A
N W E D S T O D D T O D D A F P O
I I N D N O T S N H O J I V E L I
C T E D S A R A H P A L I N X U L
T C H E L E N T H O M A S E X M M
U H C D S B D D O T O D D E O B I
R D H A I R S T Y L I S T Y N E N
I O A L V I S L I V E S D G E R I
S C N H G U A B M I L H S U R A S
T T E L A D N I J Y B B O B H S T
O Y Y T I N A F E Y T O D D A S E
D R H I G H S C H O O L B F F O R
```

Mystery Picture Answer

Finish the sentence by filling in the missing word:

1) FIRE, 2) OFFICE, 3) ROGUE, 4) ROGUE, 5) APPOINT, BUDDY, 6) WOOTEN, 7) MILLION, 8) ROGUE, 9) ROGUE

Unscramble the words and complete the sentence:

1) KUWAIT, 2) ENDANGERED, 3) ROGUE, 4) MARRIAGE, 5) CONTAMINATION, 6) CREATIONISM, 7) NATIONAL, 8) SECESSIONIST, 9) CHRISTIAN, 10) WASILLA

Crossword Puzzlin' Time

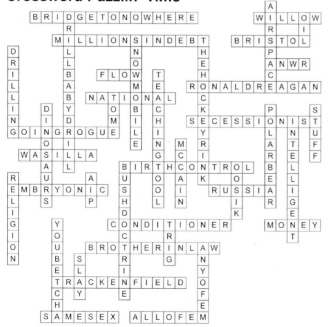

The Tao-in' of Palin

```
R O G U E I N M E N I T T I U Q T
E S H O O T I N D E E D W N D C E
S E C E D I N W A V I N I G I R L
I B A R I B A B B L I N T R S A E
G I M E V S U C K I N X T A T Z P
N T P V E D E L U D I N E C O Y R
I C A E R B L U F F I N R I R M O
C H I N T X C U T T I N I A T A M
O I G G I C O N F U S I N T I K P
N N N I N E O C O N I N Z I N I T
I I I N N S T U P I F Y I N N I E
K F N O O C A V I N I T L O V E R
N E P O T I S M I N C A S H I N I
I F R A U D I N R E V E L A T I N
W O L F K I L L I N K S L A Y I N
S P E A K I N I N T O N G U E S O
B L A B B I N H B L I T H E R I N
```

Answers

Which are not Sarah Palin's kids' names?

```
T I N A F E Y O B U D D H A O S K
W T R A C K E N F I E L D G O H I
I W P O L I T I C A L P R O P O L
T R Y B I R T H C O N T R O L T L
T A Y D B O O G A B O O G A O G A
E P G O D A I P S W I L L O W U F
R T H J E S U S H C H R I S T N R
Q H I I P A A O N A O A A I P W O
U A L I P F I O C I O I A I P E M
I T L P I P E R A P O P A I P D W
T R B I P T O O R H I L L O O D A
T A I N M Y C A R B I L L Y O I S
E S L I P E R O Y S L U S H Y N I
R C L O O F O B R I S T O L O G L
O A Y O O F O S A R A H J R I F L
D L R I C H I E R I C H T R I G A
L O C K A N D L O A D O O P R O P
```